A good time is coming, I wish it were here,
The very best time in the whole of the year;
I'm counting each day on my fingers and thumbs-
The weeks that must pass before Santa Claus comes.

Then when the first snowflakes begin to come down,
And the wind whistles sharp and the branches are brown,
I'll not mind the cold, though my fingers it numbs,
For it brings the time nearer when Santa Claus comes.

AUTHOR UNKNOWN

THE BIG BOOK OF CHRISTMAS

THE BIG BOOK OF CHRISTMAS

LAUGHING ELEPHANT · MMXIII

ISBN/EAN: 9781595836267

LAUGHING ELEPHANT

LAUGHINGELEPHANT.com

JAMES MONTGOMERY FLAGG

Preface

I have sought in this book to capture the timeless essence of Christmas. While recognizing that each person's Christmas is a little different, I believe that there is enough commonality for a gathering of words and images to be widely resonant.

My approach is primarily visual. Illustrators select single moments from the ever-shifting flow of reality and share them with us, hoping thereby to evoke the larger experience. I have the same hope. I have assembled one hundred pictures from our large library of books and ephemera, and supplemented the images of each section with quotations that explain and, hopefully, deepen the pictures.

The Big Book of Christmas is roughly arranged to show Christmas as it unfolds in time. We begin with distant anticipation of Christmas to come, pass on to children's letters to Santa, then Christmas shopping, the wrapping of gifts, and so on, through to children enjoying their presents on Christmas morning. To this narrative I have appended a section on other aspects of Christmas— the various guises of Santa Claus, Animals at Christmas, children's accidental encounters with Santa, Christmas Cards and several others.

I hope that this collection enriches your experience of this most beloved holiday.

WELLERAN POLTARNEES

Dreaming of Christmas

Perhaps, for children, the months spent anticipating the Christmas to come is the sweetest part of the season. Certainly it is the most long lasting. They hoped-for bicycle is taller and more beautiful than the real one that will be. Riding it is more effortless, and as it glides through town, in our dream, there will be no obstacles. The daydream bicycle will always be lovely and new, whereas the real one will soon grow old.

Christmas is not a date. It is a state of mind.

MARY ELLEN CHASE

1

Letters to Santa Claus

A letter to Santa Claus is drawn from deep in the mind of the child who writes one. It is a utopian vision that most of the writers know, in some part of their minds, will never come to pass, but it is wonderful to surrender wholly to dreams and desire.

There are two philosophies in writing a letter to Santa. The commonest one overstates and over-lists in the hope that Santa will give grandly when he sees how large the wishes are. The other, and craftier, approach is to make a modest list because of a suspicion that a large list will be seen as greedy, which will offend Santa and lead him to be less generous. One cannot be sure which is the better gamble.

Letters to Santa Claus are drawn from deep in the mind of the child who writes one. It is a utopian vision that most of the writers know, in some part of their minds, will never come to pass, but it is wonderful to surrender wholly to dreams and desire.

WELLERAN POLTARNEES

Letters to Santa Claus

What child has not known the inner difficulty of trying to put down on paper the "list" of desired gifts? First, perhaps, because everyone retains the hope of receiving some fabulous gift, as we have mentioned, something more precious than anything he could ever imagine. Even the child who knows very clearly what he wants still expects, more or less secretly to himself, some extraordinary surprise.

PAUL TOURNIER

Santa at Work

Santa Claus takes a time off after Christmas to rest. When he feels at full strength he opens the workshop. Most of the elves have been on ski vacations, but they sense when it is time to return and go to work. The workshop is entirely underground. It is vast and filled with leftover toys, workbenches, and new materials.

Santa Claus approves every design and spot checks the finished toys for quality. He manufactures no electronic devices, but sub-contracts them to manufacturers in various countries. Only timeless toys are made here.

While they work the elves sing joyful songs. Santa smiles and taps his foot.

ANONYMOUS

Santa at Work

Santa could presumably create his myriad gifts through magic, but he does not do so. He, and his elves, hand-craft each one. We are glad that he does this. If there were not labor involved, if he did not have to fly around the world, visiting each home, the gifts would not be as appreciated. Magic is too easy. He and his trusty elves labor all year long for the happiness of mankind.

Shopping

I love the sidewalk whiffs of roasting chestnuts, the clanging of the Salvation Army bells, the Ho! Ho! Ho's! of a hundred Santa Clauses. I love the store windows, the crowds of shoppers with their parcels, the merrymaking, three deep, in all the bars. I love the candle-lit church services that herald the birth of Jesus, and the peace that settles over the city late on Christmas Eve. And on Christmas morning, I love the cries of "Merry Christmas!" and the smiles. I love our great midwinter festival.

JOCK ELLIOTT

Your true lover of Christmas thoroughly enjoys Christmas shopping and the stores with their glowing windows. Inside the tables are heaped with treasures. Carols fall in a mist over the throngs of happy shoppers. We are all there for a single reason: the search for gifts for those we love, and we feel joined by commonality of purpose. Our quest makes an exciting game of the shopping–can we find the perfect fit for each person on our list? In retrospect we know that we cannot, but the festive hysteria of the mob makes us believe that we can.

Wrapping Gifts

This seemingly simple act is, symbolically, important. Our choice of paper tells much about us. It is tasteful? Expensive? Traditional? Are the corners folded perfectly? Was the ribbon or cord thoughtfully matched with the paper? Do we use a card or tag or label, and how do we inscribe it?

Like many aspects of Christmas, wrapping gifts is challenging and sometimes stressful, but also exciting and pleasurable if approached in the right frame of mind.

Wrapping Gifts

At Christmas time, when we are all a little childish I hope, surprise is the flavor of our keenest joys. We all remember the thrill with which we once heard, behind some closed door, the rustle and crackle of paper parcels being tied up. We knew that we were going to be surprised--a delicious refinement and luxuriant seasoning of the emotion!

CHRISTOPHER DARLINGTON MORLEY

Christmas Greenery

Christmas as it developed absorbed many pre-Christian customs and rituals. One of these is the use of greenery in the home, traditional in Roman and Scandinavian mid-winter festivals. Today we scent and beautify our homes at Christmas with nature's bounty through wreaths, holly, poinsettias and other traditional Christmas flora.

Christmas Greenery

The holly's up, the house is all bright;
The tree is ready, the candles alight:
Rejoice and be glad, all children tonight!

P. CORNELIUS

Sophie Wilson

We announce to the world, through the exterior adornment of our homes, that we are excited about the Christmas season. We want our homes to shout to all who pass by, "Merry Christmas!" The means vary— trees hung with ornaments, snowmen and snow creatures of all variety, Santa in his sleigh, candy canes and etc. Beginning in the 1930s electrical displays became possible. Most towns have homes that shine with thousands of lights. More recent developments in lighting technology have expanded the possibilities in holiday illumination to the point that light spectaculars in our yards and our rooftops are an attainable indulgence.

A wreath on the front door, its shape signifying love without beginning or end, is the perfect welcome to holiday guests.

Decorating the House

Whatever your taste may be, one thing is certain: Christmas is the time, in the matter of decoration, to let the fancy roam: to be inventive, creative, gay, light-hearted, and unafraid. I have often noticed that uninspired people, released by the Christmas spirit from fear of being criticized or laughed at, will show a taste and inventiveness — will produce decorative effects surprisingly more beautiful — than they will at other times of the year.

CONSTANCE SPRY

Most people depend upon their decorated trees to represent Christmas inside their homes, but for those in whom the Christmas spirit overflows, many other acts of decoration are possible.

Children's projects, such as popcorn and cranberry chains, paper angels and the like, are a charming addition to any room. Greenery is lovely, easy, and pleasant smelling. Nowadays lights are not just in string form, and the creative person can easily turn a home into a twinkling winter wonderland. A glass vessel filled with vintage Christmas ornaments, a tabletop or other surface covered with greeting cards, a wooden bowl filled with nuts in the shell and surrounded by beautiful candles— Christmas is the time to fill one's home with beauty.

Decorating the House

It was the day before Christmas, fifty years earlier. She and her brother Tom were trimming the Christmas tree in this very library. She saw Tom, in a white piqué suit with short socks that were always slipping down his fat legs. She saw herself in a white dress and blue ribbons, pouting in a corner. They had been quarreling about the Christmas tree, disputing as to which of them should light the first candle when the time arrived. Then their mother came to them smiling, a sweet-faced lady who seemed not to notice the red faces and the tears. She put something into Tom's hand saying, "This is the Christmas Angel of peace and good-will. Hang it on the tree, children, so that it may shed a blessing on all who come here to give and to receive."

How lovely and pink it looked in Tom's hand! Little Angelina had thought it the most beautiful thing she had ever seen,-- and holy, too, as if it had some blessed charm. Fiddlestick! What queer fancies children have! Miss Terry remembered how a strange thrill had crept through Angelina as she gazed at it. Then she and Tom looked at each other and were ashamed of their quarrel. Suddenly Tom held out the Angel to his sister. "You hang it on the tree, Angelina," he said magnanimously. "I know you want to."

ABBIE FARWELL BROWN

Choosing a Tree

The choice of a Christmas tree is complex. How early do we secure our tree, knowing that the earlier we buy the more of the season we have to enjoy it, but the later we buy it the more fragrant it will be on Christmas Day? Do our decorations look better on a full tree, or one with elegantly spaced branches? Many enjoy going to the countryside to cut their own tree, while others visit urban or suburban Christmas tree lots. Potted trees, to be planted after Christmas or even reused, are an environmentally responsible choice, as are artificial trees, which can look remarkably authentic, or delightfully kitsch.

Choosing a Tree

When I was a boy the yearly selection of a Christmas tree seemed to be of supreme importance. I started to beg my parents to buy a tree on Thanksgiving Day, and they always put me off. They claimed that the tree would dry out if purchased too early. They said that if we waited that prices would fall. I continued to nag, and about a week before Christmas they succumbed.

Sometimes we went out to the country and cut a tree. I loved this. It made me feel like a pioneer. Usually we went to a Christmas tree stand. I wanted massive trees, but my parents pointed out we had low ceilings. The best trees were always too expensive. Finally, they chose a short and inexpensive tree. When we got it home and put it up, I realized that all Christmas trees were wonderful.

HAROLD DARLING

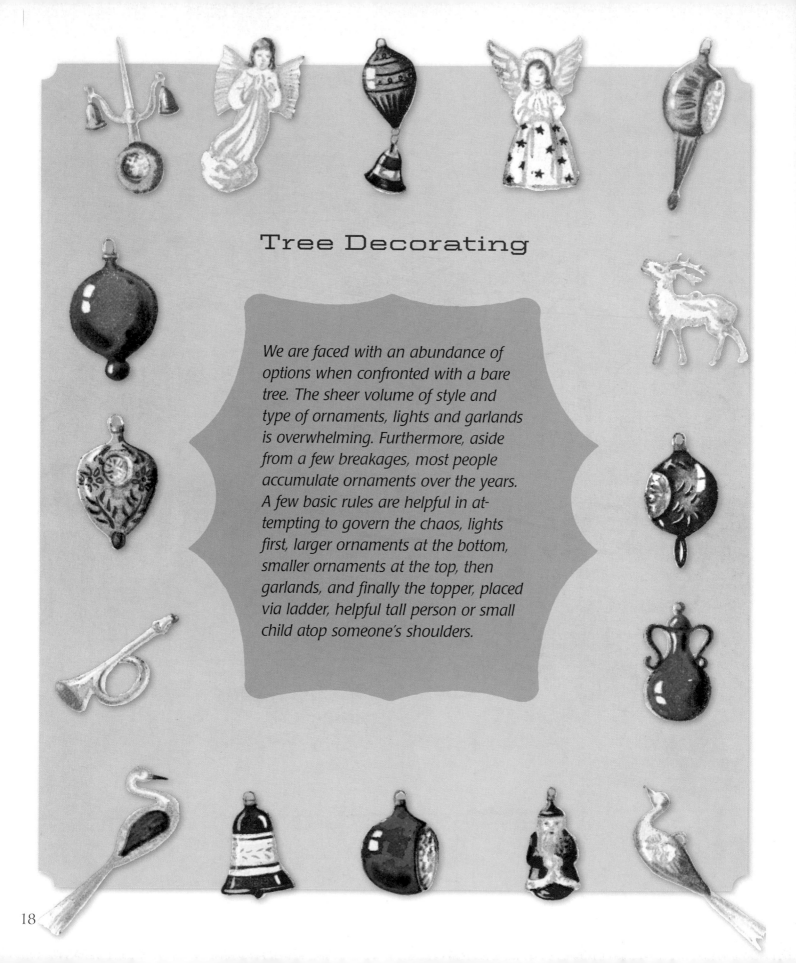

Tree Decorating

We are faced with an abundance of options when confronted with a bare tree. The sheer volume of style and type of ornaments, lights and garlands is overwhelming. Furthermore, aside from a few breakages, most people accumulate ornaments over the years. A few basic rules are helpful in attempting to govern the chaos, lights first, larger ornaments at the bottom, smaller ornaments at the top, then garlands, and finally the topper, placed via ladder, helpful tall person or small child atop someone's shoulders.

Tree Decorating

Choose wisely then, each ornament.
And frosted tinsel skein.
For braches that have worn jewels
Of gleaming mountain rain.

ELIZABETH-ELLAN LONG

Resplendent stands the glitt'ring tree
Weighted with gifts for all to see.

ANNE P.L. FIELD

O! Christmas tree— what art thou but a symbol of the promise
of life— laden with the desires of our hearts. Everyone finds
in it his own desire, which he may grasp with his own hands.
But— all these various desires are illusions— which conceal our
deepest and purest desire— the desire for LIGHT. Every soul is
attracted to this mysterious tree— we are born with this innate
craving for LIGHT.

HENRIETTE WILLEBEEK LE MAIR

Christmas waves a magic wand over
this world and behold, everything is
softer and more beautiful.

NORMAN VINCENT PEALE

The Christmas Tree

The Christmas tree was brought from the hemlock woods. Then one waited forever and forever while it was changed to a magic tree with shining balls and candles.

TASHA TUDOR

Christmas
Eve

Is there any more enduring, cherished reminder of the halcyon days of our childhood than the Christmas stocking? For one night each year that otherwise ordinary article of clothing is miraculously transformed into a captivating catchall— hung empty, by the fireplace before bedtime, and retrieved gleefully at the crack of dawn, bulging with Santa's bounty.

MERYLE EVANS

Christmas Eve

For children the anticipation of Christmas grows stronger every day, culminating in the nearly unbearable waiting that Christmas Eve entails.

Sleep is difficult for the entire family. Children fight to remain awake, listening. Was that the thud of Santa's sleigh? Several checks may be made to see if Santa has eaten his cookies, or the reindeer their carrots. The family pets are excited and confused. Beleaguered parents struggle to keep their children in bed and finally, out of sheer exhaustion, everyone falls asleep, dreaming of the morning's delights.

Christmas Eve

Fireplaces are symbols of comfort. In earlier times they were a principal means of heat and cooking. They are places where we sit to relax and enjoy the ever-changing beauty of flame. At Christmastime they are frequently the place where Christmas stockings are hung, and, of course, the traditional entry for Santa Claus into our homes.

Christmas Eve was a night of song that wrapped itself about you like a shawl. But it warmed more than your body. It warmed your heart...filled it, too, with melody that would last forever.

BESS STREETER

Christmas Eve

So it is that Christmas Eve is the best part of Christmas. Compared with the clamor and urgency of the day itself—the schedules to satisfy, the near-strangers to pretend to be close to, the post-gift frenzy to compare windfalls—Christmas Eve is serene. It is the moment, still and expectant, when the warmth of the season may be felt for its own sake—the moment to light candles and listen for a sound in the distance. It is the moment when the meaning of the day, for those who wonder at it, may be contemplated without distraction from timetables or remote-controlled robots.

GREGG EASTERBROOK

Santa Arrives!

Different cultures explain Santa's visit in various ways. He travels by horse or donkey; he walks, pulling a sleigh, he has angels to help him. Scandinavia and the United States visualize him in a flying sleigh pulled by reindeer. This is a delightful image, and one that has greatly inspired artists and illustrators.

Santa Arrives!

The moon shone big and white in the sky, and the snow lay crisp and sparkling on the ground as Santa Claus cracked his whip and sped away out of the Valley into the great world beyond. The roomy sleigh was packed full with huge sacks of toys, and as the reindeer dashed onward our jolly old Santa laughed and whistled and sang for very joy. For in all his merry life this was the one day in the year when he was happiest--the day he lovingly bestowed the treasures of his workshop upon the little children.

It would be a busy night for him, he well knew. As he whistled and shouted and cracked his whip again, he reviewed in mind all the towns and cities and farmhouses where he was expected, and figured that he had just enough presents to go around and make every child happy. The reindeer knew exactly what was expected of them, and dashed along so swiftly that their feet scarcely seemed to touch the snow-covered ground.

L. FRANK BAUM

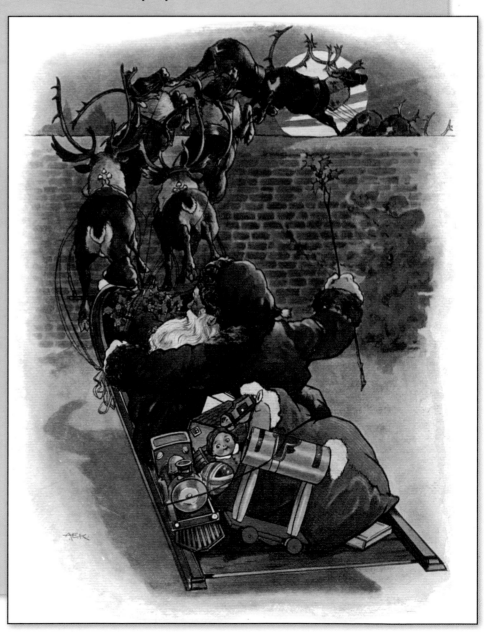

Santa Arrives!

Clement Moore will always be an immortal, not only for his memorable summary of Santa's visit in "The Night Before Christmas" but also because he first told us the names of the reindeer:

"Now Dasher! now, Dancer! now, Prancer and Vixen!

On, Comet! On, Cupid! on, on Donner and Blitzen!"

Santa Arrives!

Here Santa Claus was driving his reindeer, his teeming sleigh filled with wonders from every region: dolls that walked and talked and sang, fit for princesses; sleds fine enough for princes; drums and trumpets and swords for young heroes; horses that looked as though they were alive and would spring next moment from their rockers; bats and balls that almost started of themselves from their places; little uniforms, and frocks; skates; tennis-racquets; baby caps and rattles; tiny engines and coaches; railway trains; animals that ran about; steamships; books; pictures—everything to delight the soul of childhood and gratify the affection of age.

THOMAS NELSON PAGE

Down the Chimney

The rational mind worries about Santa's traditional way of entering homes. He is seemingly too large for almost every chimney, and what about his bags? What about chimney covers and baffles and flues? What if there is a fire? He might be soiled with soot? What about children who live in places lacking chimneys?

But of course, Santa is a magician.

Down the Chimney

LEAP, Santa, down our chimney
With all-embracing fervour
In boots and beard so comely
Be now the red-checked saviour,
Volcano out your lava,

Where mixed with father's braces
And box of chocs for mother
Meccano sets build kisses
Where gliders lover each other
And sister flatters brother.

Dish out a world where tinsel
Spells laughter out in streamers
And gift propelling-pencil
Makes poems up for dreamers
And writes all wrong for schemers.

The chance we had the feeling
Was ours just for the knocking
Before we started quailing
At warnings old but shocking:
Just drop it in the stocking.

JOHN WAIN

All the house was asleep,
And the fire burning low,
When, from far up the chimney,
Came down a "Ho! Ho!"

MRS. C.S. STONE

33

Santa's Here!

His droll little mouth was drawn up like a bow,
And the beard of his chin was as white as the snow.

The stump of a pipe he held tight in his teeth,
And the smoke it encircled his head like a wreath.

CLEMENT C. MOORE

Treats left for Santa and the reindeer are a wonderful addition to the Christmas mythology. We are of course grateful to Santa Claus, but finding a gift for the ultimate gift-giver— and someone who probably has everything— is a monumentally difficult task. Homemade cookies are always welcome, and appreciated on a busy night. The reindeer get hungry as well, and enjoy the apples and carrots left out for them.

Santa Claus could just leave a big pack of gifts in the middle of the room but he does not do this because he clearly has an aesthetic appreciation of arrangement and he knows that we will appreciate thoughtfully placed gifts.

Santa and the Toys

Was there ever a wider and more loving conspiracy than that which keeps the venerable figure of Santa Claus from slipping away with all of the other old-time myths, into the forsaken wonderland of the past?

HAMILTON WRIGHT MABIE

The more anyone retains of the childlike nature, the more one is likely to enjoy the company of children. Santa Claus clearly favors children so we may conclude that he still has much of the child's love of play. Despite the burden of responsibility on Christmas Eve, he still finds a boy's delight in playing with some of his gifts.

Santa and the Toys

Santa Claus, with the help of his elves, has personally manufactured many of the toys he delivers. Despite the changes he has seen in Christmas over the years, he still feels enormous pride in everything that passes through his hands.

HAROLD DARLING

Christmas Morning

Christmas is the day that holds all time together.

ALEXANDER SMITH

For each of us the high points of life are different and individual. For one it may be falling in love, or the birth of their first child, or some act of recognition. For others it might be a mountain summit attained, or professional accomplishment, or an artistic vision achieved. For many children, for whom time moves so much more slowly, a high point of their year is Christmas morning.

Christmas Morning

There was the feeling which always came with Christmas,
that the adult world had come to its senses and done
away with all that was dull.

CLARE BOYLAN

Christmas Morning

I do not see how any child
Is cross on Christmas day
When all the lovely toys are new,
And anyone can play.

KATHERINE PYLE

Christmas Morning

Christmas! The very word brings joy to our hearts. No matter how we may dread the rush, the long Christmas lists for gifts and cards to be bought and given--when Christmas Day comes there is still the same warm feeling we had as children, the same warmth that enfolds our hearts and our homes.

JOAN WINMILL BROWN

Hooray! Hooray! It's Christmas Day,
And Santa Claus has been this way!
Just look at all the things I've got
He's left me such a lovely lot!

MURIEL DAWSON

Christmas Morning

There are few times in each of our lives when the cup of joy is so full that the joy overflows. For children Christmas is a time of such abundance. The toys are better than they had dreamed, they are surrounded with people sharing their happiness. The whole day lies before them without a cloud of worry or duty. They float in a state of bliss.

There's nothing sadder in this world than to awake Christmas morning and not be a child.

ERMA BOMBECK

Christmas Morning

Were I a philosopher, I should write a philosophy of toys, showing that nothing else in life need to be taken seriously, and that Christmas Day in the company of children is one of the few occasions on which men become entirely alive.

ROBERT LYND

Sometimes Christmas Day brings children a version of the joys and responsibilities of parenthood. There may be toy animals and dolls to care for, and it is touching how tenderly they treat their new charges.

Christmas Morning

Small gifts have a magic of their own. Bicycles and video games are thrilling, but the tokens found in Christmas stockings, or hanging from the tree, are wonderful additions to the holiday tumult. They are piquant additions, like nuts sprinkled on an ice cream sundae.

Christmas Morning

Annie Benson Müller

In that instant, above all, when nothing yet had been taken from the tree, when all the candles burned and no cautious hand had been stretched out to take even one of them away, when the whole evening lay ahead, and beyond the evening, sleep that would end on Christmas morning, a child's mind held within itself the pleasure of fulfillment and expectation in perfect equipoise, as it could not have done if he had been a receiver or spectator only, if he himself had not contributed to this festival and built it with his hands and mind.

CHARLES MORGAN

Christmas Morning

Like the eye of the storm, the still center in the midst of a hurricane, there often comes on Christmas Day a brief moment of calm, when the children stop in the midst of their excitement and sit in wonder at their bounty and the pleasant times yet to come.

Christmas Carols

Everything was quiet; everywhere there was the faint crackling silence of the winter night. We started singing, and we were all moved by the words and the sudden trueness of our voices. Pure, very clear, and breathless we sang.

LAURIE LEE

Christmas Carols

The Christmas Carol has complex roots, partly in the spirit of St. Francis of Assisi. He combined mirthfulness, childish simplicity and emotional fervor, and in so doing transformed the hymn into what we now know as Christmas carols. Another early developer of the form was John Awdlay, a 15th century British priest.

Nowell, Nowell, Nowell,
Nowell, sing all we may
Because the King of all kings
Was born this blessed day.

At Church

Loving Father, help us remember the birth of Jesus, that we may share in the song of the angels, the gladness of the shepherds, and worship of the wise men.

Close the door of hate and open the door of love all over the world. Let kindness come with every gift and good desires with every greeting. Deliver us from evil by the blessing which Christ brings, and teach us to be merry with clear hearts.

May the Christmas morning make us happy to be thy children, and Christmas evening bring us to our beds with grateful thoughts, forgiving and forgiven, for Jesus' sake.

Amen!

ROBERT LOUIS STEVENSON

55

JOHN MARTIN'S LETTER
To Very Little Boys and Girls

DEAR LITTLE FRIENDS

I AM SO GLAD that it is really *true* that I am sitting down again to have a talk with *you*. You see, my letter starts right in to talk to you in RHYME. My letter is a sort of SONG, because it's CHRISTMAS-TIME. It seems to me that Christmas-time must give some HAPPY THING that goes right *into* all our hearts and makes us *want* to sing. Yes, Dears, there is a "Happy Thing," for it is LOVE, of course, and love is just another name for loving SANTA CLAUS. This living, *loving* Santa Claus has *many* happy faces, and he is "magic", so he *lives* in many thousand Places. *Especially* at Christmas-time, he goes around and gives, a thousand-*thousand* precious GIFTS to every thing that lives. He goes to little CHILDREN'S hearts and whispers happy words. He even slips into the hearts of Animals and Birds. He tells us to be *happy*, and he shows us what to do to give some LOVE and HAPPINESS to other people too. He tells us that on Christmas Day we never should *forget*, that there are many things to GIVE as well as things to *get*. At Christmas-time he brings such lots of LOVE and LIFE and CHEER, that he expects us to be good and HAPPY for a *year*. O, yes, he loves you and my Dears, Your Fathers and Your Mothers Know all about the Love he gives and so do hosts of others. And O, he wants to have you be his LITTLE HELPERS too, because at Christmas-time he has so many things to *do*. Yes, you can help dear Santa Claus by *giving* LOVE away. He cannot get along without your help on Christmas Day. So, Dearies, HELP him all you can, then You will be a part of all the JOY of Christmas-time and of his loving Heart. As for my "MERRY CHRISTMAS" Dears, I WISH that you may see the best and *dearest* CHRISTMAS GIFTS upon your Christmas Tree. And then I ask dear Santa Claus to stay around and give you HEALTH, and LOVE, and HAPPINESS FOR ALL THE DAYS YOU LIVE.

John-Martin

And HERE COME CHRISTMAS GREETINGS and LOVE from

Merry Christmas FROM Quizzy Bear

HO-NEY

I WISH FOR YOU A LOT OF TOYS,
THAT *TOOT* AND *SQUEAK*
AND MAKE A NOISE.
I WISH FOR YOU SOME STICKY HONEY
AND, (IF YOU WANT IT,) LOTS OF MONEY,
AND THEN, I WISH YOU LOTS OF *FUN*
AND PLEASANT SNOOZES IN THE SUN.
ALL THESE SHALL "HAPPY CHRISTMAS" BRING YOU,
WITH NOT ONE naughty BEE TO STING YOU.
YOUR LOVING "QUIZZY"

A HAPPY CHRISTMAS from BUMP Your DOG

I WISH MY TAIL WAS VERY *LONG*,
(AT LEAST A YARD OR TWO,)
SO I COULD WAG A BIG LONG WAG,
ACROSS THE WORLD TO YOU:
BUT I WILL WAG MY LITTLE TAIL,
AND EVERY WAG SHALL BE
A "MERRY, MERRY CHRISTMAS WAG",
JUST *FULL* OF LOVE FROM ME,
from Your little Friend

MY BIG HEART

Bump

A JOLLY CHRISTMAS from WOBBIE CHUBBIE

GOOD FORTUNE

SEND YOU A BUSHEL OF
LAUGHS AND FUN, AND A BOX
OF LOVE AND *TOYS*,
SO, LAUGH AND SCAMPER,
AND ROMP, AND RUN, LIKE
HAPPY GIRLS AND BOYS.
I WISH YOU A MERRY CHRISTMAS DAY, WITH
HEALTH, AND JOY AND LAUGHTER. AND
NOTHING SHALL COME TO TAKE AWAY THE
JOY OF YOUR DAYS HEREAFTER
FROM YOUR WOBBIE

CHRISTMAS GREETINGS from WINNIE CHUBBIE

ONE AND ONE MAKE 2,
TWO AND TWO MAKE 4,
KEEP ON ADDING TO THAT SUM
MANY THOUSANDS MORE.
WHEN YOU GET IT DONE—
WHEN YOUR SUM IS THROUGH,
IT WILL BE THE ANSWER FOR
ALL I WISH FOR YOU WHEN I WISH AND WISH,
WHILE YOU'RE WISHING TOO; DON'T YOU
THINK THAT WE CAN MAKE EVERY
WISH COME TRUE? DO Winnie

GOOD LUCK TO YOU

B WELL

SAM A FRED
JOLLY CHRISTMAS

B HAPPY   B GOOD

DAN A TIM
A HAPPY NEW YEAR

How many pictures can you find?

THE TWELVE DAYS OF CHRISTMAS

A Traditional English Folk Song

ON the First Day of Christmas
my true love sent to me
a partridge in a pear tree.

ON the Second Day of Christmas
my true love sent to me
two turtle-doves, and a partridge in a pear tree.

ON the Third Day of Christmas
my true love sent to me
three French hens, two turtle-doves, and a
partridge in a pear tree.

ON the Fourth Day of Christmas
my true love sent to me
four calling birds, three French hens, two turtle-
doves, and a partridge in a pear tree.

ON the Fifth Day of Christmas
my true love sent to me
five gold rings, four calling birds, three French
hens, two turtle-doves, and a partridge in a
pear tree.

ON the Sixth Day of Christmas
my true love sent to me
six geese a-laying, five gold rings, four calling
birds, three French hens, two turtle-doves, and
a partridge in a pear tree.

ON the Seventh Day of Christmas
my true love sent to me
seven swans a-swimming, six geese a-laying, five
gold rings, four calling birds, three French hens,
two turtle-doves, and a partridge in a pear tree.

ON the Eighth Day of Christmas
my true love sent to me

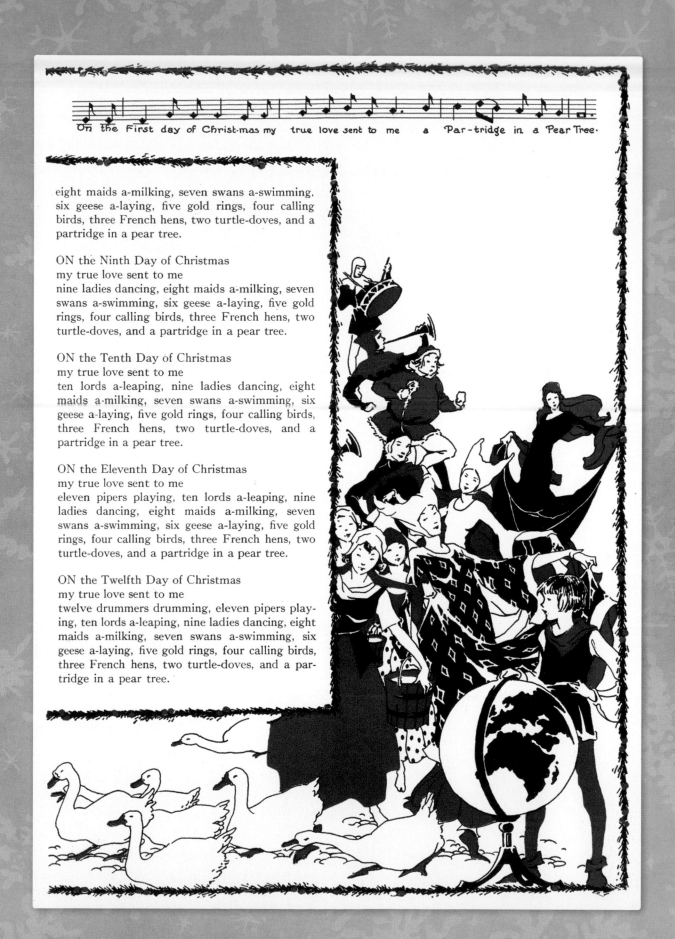

On the First day of Christmas my true love sent to me a Partridge in a Pear Tree.

eight maids a-milking, seven swans a-swimming, six geese a-laying, five gold rings, four calling birds, three French hens, two turtle-doves, and a partridge in a pear tree.

ON the Ninth Day of Christmas
my true love sent to me
nine ladies dancing, eight maids a-milking, seven swans a-swimming, six geese a-laying, five gold rings, four calling birds, three French hens, two turtle-doves, and a partridge in a pear tree.

ON the Tenth Day of Christmas
my true love sent to me
ten lords a-leaping, nine ladies dancing, eight maids a-milking, seven swans a-swimming, six geese a-laying, five gold rings, four calling birds, three French hens, two turtle-doves, and a partridge in a pear tree.

ON the Eleventh Day of Christmas
my true love sent to me
eleven pipers playing, ten lords a-leaping, nine ladies dancing, eight maids a-milking, seven swans a-swimming, six geese a-laying, five gold rings, four calling birds, three French hens, two turtle-doves, and a partridge in a pear tree.

ON the Twelfth Day of Christmas
my true love sent to me
twelve drummers drumming, eleven pipers playing, ten lords a-leaping, nine ladies dancing, eight maids a-milking, seven swans a-swimming, six geese a-laying, five gold rings, four calling birds, three French hens, two turtle-doves, and a partridge in a pear tree.

Despite a lack of biblical evidence, it has long been believed that an ox and an ass were present at Christ's birth. It is appropriate, then, that we should want to include our animal friends in the holiday that celebrates that event, and especially apropos that we should want them present in this season of love.

Animals at Christmas

Dogs and cats are humankind's closest companions. They must be surprised and mystified by our holiday preparations, all the hustle and bustle of preparations and wrapping paper and admonitions to stay out of the way, but they understand the feasting, the comradeship and the joy that Christmastime brings.

Animals at Christmas

Bread and milk for breakfast
And woolen frocks to wear,
And a crumb for Robin Redbreast
On the cold days of the year.

CHRISTINA ROSSETTI

In Boston's Post Office Square in the 1920s the SPCA used to erect a horses' Christmas tree. On Christmas Eve the few draft animals remaining in the business district gathered around to nibble apples and sugar lumps from the tree. Pennsylvania farmers similarly put up trees in their barnyards, decorating them with carrots and cabbages and other things animals like to eat.

PHILLIP SNYDER

The Friendly Beasts

Jesus our brother, strong and good,
Was humbly born in a stable rude,
And the friendly beasts around Him stood,
Jesus our brother, strong and good.

"I," said the donkey shaggy and brown,
"I carried His mother up hill and down,
I carried her safely to Bethlehem town;
I," said the donkey, shaggy and brown.

"I," said the cow all white and red,
"I gave Him my manger for His bed,
I gave Him my hay to pillow His head,
I," said the cow all white and red.

"I," said the sheep with curly horn,
"I gave Him my wool for His blanket warm,
He wore my coat on Christmas morn;
I," said the sheep with curly horn.

"I," said the dove, from the rafters high,
"Cooed Him to sleep, my mate and I,
We cooed Him to sleep, my mate and I;
I," said the dove, from the rafters high.

And every beast, by some good spell,
In the stable dark was glad to tell,
Of the gift he gave Immanuel,
The gift he gave Immanuel.

     (Twelfth-Century Carol)

'Twas the Night before Christmas

When all through the house, not a creature was stirring, not even a mouse, The Stockings were hung by the chimney with care, In the hopes that St. Nicholas soon would be there. The children were nestled all snug in their beds while visions of sugar-plums danced in their heads, and mama in her 'kerchief and I in my cap had just settled our brains for a long winter's nap, when out on the lawn there arose such a clatter I sprang from the bed to see what was the matter. * * * * * Away to the window I flew like a flash, tore open the shutters and threw up the sash. * * * * The moon on the breast of the new-fallen snow gave the lustre of mid-day to objects below, when, what to my wondering eyes should appear but a miniature sleigh and eight tiny reindeer, with a little old driver, so lively and quick, I knew in a moment it must be St. Nick. * * * More rapid than eagles, his coursers they came, and he whistled and shouted, and called them by name. "Now, Dasher! Now, Dancer! Now, Prancer and Vixen. On, Comet! On, Cupid! On, Donder and Blitzen! To the top of the porch, to the top of the wall! * * * Now dash away, dash away, dash away all!" As dry leaves that before the hurricane fly, when they meet with an obstacle, mount to the sky. * * * So up to the house-top the coursers they flew, with the sleigh full of toys and St. Nicholas, too.

AND THEN IN A TWINKLING I HEARD ON THE ROOF THE
PRANCING AND PAWING OF EACH LITTLE HOOF.
AS I DREW IN MY HEAD AND WAS TURNING AROUND,
DOWN THE CHIMNEY ST. NICHOLAS CAME WITH A
BOUND. * * *
HE WAS DRESSED ALL IN FUR FROM HIS HEAD TO HIS FOOT.
AND HIS CLOTHES WERE ALL TARNISHED WITH ASHES
AND SOOT. * * * * * * * *
A BUNDLE OF TOYS HE HAD FLUNG FROM HIS BACK, AND HE
LOOKED LIKE A PEDDLER JUST OPENING HIS PACK.
HIS EYES, HOW THEY TWINKLED! HIS DIMPLES, HOW MERRY!
HIS CHEEKS WERE LIKE ROSES, HIS NOSE LIKE A
CHERRY! HIS DROLL LITTLE MOUTH WAS DRAWN UP LIKE
A BOW, AND THE BEARD OF HIS CHIN WAS AS WHITE AS THE
SNOW, THE STUMP OF A PIPE HE HELD TIGHT IN HIS TEETH,
AND THE SMOKE IT ENCIRCLED HIS HEAD LIKE A WREATH,
HE HAD A BROAD FACE AND A LITTLE ROUND BELLY THAT
SHOOK WHEN HE LAUGHED LIKE A BOWL FULL OF JELLY.
HE WAS CHUBBY AND PLUMP, A RIGHT JOLLY OLD ELF, AND
I LAUGHED WHEN I SAW HIM IN SPITE OF MYSELF. * *
A WINK OF HIS EYE AND A TWIST OF HIS HEAD SOON GAVE
ME TO KNOW I HAD NOTHING TO DREAD. * * * *
HE SPOKE NOT A WORD, BUT WENT STRAIGHT TO HIS WORK
AND FILLED ALL THE STOCKINGS, THEN TURNED WITH A JERK.
AND LAYING HIS FINGER ASIDE OF HIS
NOSE, AND GIVING A NOD, UP THE CHIMNEY
HE ROSE. HE SPRANG TO HIS SLEIGH, TO HIS TEAM GAVE
A WHISTLE, AND AWAY THEY
ALL FLEW LIKE THE DOWN
OF A THISTLE.
BUT I HEARD HIM EXCLAIM ERE HE DROVE OUT OF SIGHT,
"HAPPY CHRISTMAS TO ALL, AND TO ALL A GOODNIGHT."

The Same to You

Santa with the Children

It is only natural that children would hope to catch at least a glimpse of Santa Claus. His largesse is so important to them, and his powers so astonishing that, even though they have seen pictures, they want to see this wonderful being with their own eyes.

Illustrators, who were once children themselves, satisfy this unfulfilled hope (for Santa is wily) by frequently picturing Santa encountering people on his Christmas Eve duties, and even mingling with them.

Santa with the Children

He comes in the night! He comes in the night!
He softly, silently comes,

While the little brown heads on the pillows so white
Are dreaming of bugles and drums.

He cuts thro' the snow like a ship thro' the foam,
While the white flakes 'round him whirl.

Who tells him I know not, but he findeth the home
Of each good little boy and girl.

ANONYMOUS

There is a widespread desire to see Santa Claus in the flesh. During the holidays Santa Claus appears as a fundraiser and at malls and department stores for photo opportunities. These are noble efforts, but only the youngest children are convinced that this is the "real" Santa Claus. Sometimes a Christmas gathering will feature a game older gentleman in a Santa Claus costume, distributing gifts to children, but again this is an enjoyable delusion. What we really want, and will never achieve, is the real Santa Claus, laughing, talking, and mingling with us like an old friend.

The Many Faces of Santa Claus

Just what the Saint looks like is not altogether certain, but there is a belief among the children who have sat up to receive his visits that he is not so big but that he can get through an ordinary chimney; that he is compelled to dress in furs because of the cold ride through the long winter night, that he looks good-natured because no one that loves young folk can help looking so; and that his beard and his hair are white because he is older by some years than he was in his younger days.

FROM ST. NICHOLAS MAGAZINE

There is, around the world, a great variety of ways in which Christmas gifts arrive. We have angels, nanny goats, a gentle grandmother, Santa's wife, elves,— even the Christ child himself delivering gifts. In this book we are concerned solely with Santa Claus. But even here we have great variety. He can be tiny or huge. He may be in his original bishop's robes. He may be a countryman in rough winter clothes, he may dress in various colors, but usually he is large, jolly and clad in red.

The Many Faces of Santa Claus

It was a much-changed St. Nicholas which the Dutch settlers brought to the United States. Auld tells us that in the New World his pale face had become like a rosy apple. The lean ascetic is now a fat, jolly old fellow, more humanist than saint. Laying aside his canonical robes, his miter, and his pastoral staff, he has chosen an ermine-trimmed red cap and suit. He has traded his old gray mare for reindeer and sleigh.

ALFRED HOTTES

Let's dance and sing and make good cheer
For Christmas comes but once a year

G. MCFARREN

Christmas Cards

CHRISTMAS GREETING — WITH BEST LOVE.

The first Christmas card was published in England in 1843 and remarkably bore the ideal greeting: "A Merry Christmas and a Happy New Year To You." It was painted by the artist John Callcott Horsley and commissioned by Henry Cole, one of the pioneers of the British postal system.

It took more than twenty years for the idea to catch on, and though there were ups and downs, the practice of sending cards at Christmas became ever more popular through the 19th and 20th centuries and continues to the present day.

78

A
MERRY CHRISTMAS
GREETING!
To show that happy
thoughts of you
Are mine, as Christmastime comes due.

MERRY CHRISTMAS!

In the United States mass publication and distribution of Christmas Cards burgeoned at around the same time as in Great Britain— the late 19th and early 20th centuries. By the 1920s the sending of cards became a routine family obligation. Friends, relatives and business associates were added to the Christmas card list. Many families maintained lists of one hundred or more. Frequently, personalized cards were ordered from a stationer. While the custom has declined somewhat over the years, many people still send a yearly Christmas card, and nearly everyone enjoys receiving one.

A merry, merry CHRISTMAS, DEAR.

Merry Christmas
And after it's gone
May happiness
stay with you
On and on

Christmas Cards

The message the Christmas card carries is a universal one, significant both to those who believe in Christ and to those who do not. Whether it travels in religious dress, or in gay, holiday attire, or in a combination of both, it brings joy, sunshine, and happiness to a world ever in need of it. With but little regard for the miles between, it annually renews old acquaintances, cements old friendships, and brings loved ones closer.

ERNEST CHASE

GREETINGS

BEST WISHES

CHRISTMAS MEMORIES of YOU

In the dead of winter there are few blossoms with which to adorn our homes, but just then a rain of Christmas cards falls and our rooms are made bright with their color and cheer.

WELLERAN POLTARNEES

Picture Credits

Front Cover	Sarah Stilwell Weber.	Magazine cover, 1917.
Endpapers	Harold Sichel	John Martin's Book, 1921.
Half-title	Ludwig Richter	Book illustration, n.d.
Frontispiece	Anonymous	Magazine cover, 1917.
Title Page	Anonymous	Magazine cover, c. 1920.
VIII	James Montgomery Flagg	Magazine cover, 1907.
X	Anonymous	Advertising card, n.d.
1	Honor Appleton	From The Big Book of Pictures and Stories, c. 1920.
2	Anonymous	"A Bright and Happy Christmas," n.d.
3	Robert J. Wildhack	Magazine cover, 1912.
4	E. Boyd Smith	From Santa Claus and All About Him, 1908.
5	Anonymous	From Doings of Kris Kringle, 1897.
6	J.P. Miller	Magazine illustration, n.d.
7	Anonymous	Magazine illustratio, 1939.
8	Anonymous	From Art Stories for Young Children, 1933.
9	Clarence Biers	From Peter's Family, 1935.
10	E. Stuart Hardy	From Merry Folk, 1902.
11	Sophie Wilson	Magazine cover, 1929.
12	F. Sands Brunner	Magazine cover, 1933.
13	Walter Crane	From Legends for Lionel, 1887.
14	Anonymous	Advertising illustration, c. 1950.
15	Harry Anderson	Magazine cover, 1948.
16	Charles Dye	Magazine cover, 1936.
17	Edna Potter	From In Storm and Sunshine, 1938.
18	Anonymous	From The New Learning Numbers, 1957.
19	Maginel Wright Barney	Magazine illustration, 1930.
20	Clarence Biers	Magazine illustration, 1931.
21	Reinhold Nägele	Greeting card, n.d.
22-23	H. Willebeek Le Mair	Magazine illustration, 1924.
24	Anne Anderson	From Fireside Stories, 1922.
25	M.M. Gell	From Storyland, c. 1920.
26	Jessie Willcox Smith	Magazine cover, 1906.
27	Maginel Wright Barney	Magazine cover, 1936.
28-29	A.E. Kennedy	From The Night Before Christmas, 1918.
30	Anonymous	From Father Tuck's Annual, c. 1900.
31	Mabel Lucie Attwell	From Cat's Cradle, 1925.
32	Anonymous	Greeting card, n.d.
33	Joseph Cummings Chase	From The Night Before Christmas, 1913.
34	Frances Brundage	From The Night Before Christmas, 1927.
35	Charles R. Showalter	Magazine illustration, 1946.
36	Robert Skemp	Magazine cover, 1938.
37	Frances Brundage	From The Night Before Christmas, 1927.
38	B. Geyser	From The Night Before Christmas, c. 1860.
39	Anonymous	Magazine illustration, 1961.
40	Lore Friedrich-Gronau	From Alle Jahre wieder, 1935.

Picture Credits

41	Guy Hoff	Magazine cover, 1921.
42	Alice Beach Winter	Magazine cover, 1928.
43	Rosa C. Petherick	From Our New Story Book, c. 1910.
44	Muriel Dawson	From Happy Hours Picture Book, c. 1920.
45	Sarah S. Stilwell Weber	From Kiddie-Kar Book, 1920.
46	C. Twelvetrees	Magazine cover, 1934.
47	Anonymous	Magazine cover, 1933.
48	Gertrud Caspari	König ist unser Kind, 1910.
49	A.L. Bowley	From Father Tuck's Annual, c. 1910.
50	Sarah S. Stilwell	Magazine illustration, n.d.
51	Annie Benson Müller	Magazine cover, 1922.
52	S.B. Pearse	Magazine cover, 1928.
53	Treyer Evans	From The Golden Book of Carols, 1948.
54	Norman Rockwell	Advertisement, 1959.
55	Anonymous	Magazine illustration, 1924.
56	Anonymous	Magazine illustration, 1911
57	Frank Bellew	Magazine illustration, 1877.
58-59	Decie Merwin	Magazine illustration, 1931.
60	Yale Gracey	Magazine cover, 1950.
61	Anonymous	Scherenschnitte design, n.d.
62	Philip Vinton Clayton	Magazine illustration, 1919.
63	Cicely M. Barker	From Blackie's Children's Annual, 1927.
64	Anonymous	Magazine cover, 1952.
65	Else Wenz-Viëtor	From Weihnachten, 1932.
66	Wanda Gag	"Christmas Tree and Cats," n.d.
67	Anonymous	Book illustration, n.d.
68-69	Anonymous	Greeting card, n.d.
70	Anonymous	From Patridge's Children's Annual, c. 1911.
71	Anonymous	Magazine illustration, 1931.
72	Lizzie Mack	From Old Father Christmas, c. 1880.
73	Rex Whistler	"Father Christmas," c. 1939
74	(UR) Anonymous	Postcard, n.d.
	(LL) Thomas Nast	Magazine illustration, c. 1865.
	(LR) Arthur Rackham	From The Night Before Christmas, 1931
75	Else Wenz-Viëtor	From St. Nicholas in Trouble, n.d.
76	(UL) Anonymous	Postcard, c. 1912.
	(UR) Anonymous	Victorian scrap, n.d.
	(LL) Ernst Kreidolf	Postcard, c. 1920
	(LR) Anonymous	Postcard, n.d.
77	Anonymous	Book illustration, n.d.
78-79	Anonymous	Greeting cards, n.d.
Back Cover	Charles Broughton	Magazine illustration, n.d.